Play Card Games in ENGLISH

Marie-Thérèse Bougard
Illustrations by Stu McLellan

Merci à Angèle, Annabel, Savva et Théo

Contents

How to use this book	inside front cover
Card games	2-3
Card ideas	3
Card tricks	4-7
Word list	8
Cards to cut out	pull-out section
Fruit	
Wild animals	
Farm animals	
Weather	
Family	
Clothes	
Transport	
Summary cards	

b small publishing
www.bsmall.co.uk

Card games

Happy Families

Number of players: two to four people
You will need: the picture cards and the summary cards

Each player takes seven picture cards, and the leftover cards are kept in a pile. The aim of the game is to collect as many complete sets of eight picture cards as possible. Players take it in turns to ask another player for a card needed to complete a set.

Place the summary cards on the table in the centre of the game so you can refer to them to know what other cards you need to complete a family.

Memory game

Number of players: two to four people
You will need: the word cards and picture cards for two complete sets

Shuffle the cards and place them face down in four rows.

The aim of the game is to collect as many pairs as possible (a pair is a picture card and a matching word card). Player 1 turns two cards up. If they match, the player keeps the pair and has another go. If they don't match, the cards are turned back over and the next player has a go, and so on until all cards have been collected.

The winner is the person with the largest number of pairs.

Snap!

Number of players: two to four people

You will need: all of the word cards and the picture cards

Shuffle the cards and deal them out as equally as possible. Players do not look at their cards and keep them face down in a pile in front of them. The aim of the game is to end up with all the cards. In turn, players flip over the card at the top of their pile. If it is from the same set as another face-up card, the first player to say SNAP collects both piles and places them face down under their own pile.

The winner is the person who ends up with all the cards.

Card ideas

Make some additional families to play with. Here are some ideas:

Colours
red
blue
yellow
orange
purple
black
pink
white

Shapes
square
circle
triangle
rectangle
hexagon
crescent
rainbow
pyramid

Food and drink
eggs
cheese
ice-cream
bread
banana
water
orange juice
hot chocolate

Numbers
one 1
two 2
three 3
four 4
five 5
six 6
seven 7
eight 8

At the beach
sunglasses
sun umbrella
sun cream
sandcastle
fish
rubber ring
seagull
ball

1 Use all the cards apart from the summary cards. Make them into a pack and ask your friend to choose a card at random and to look at it without showing you.

Choose a card.

Look at the card.

2 Ask your friend to put the card back on top of the pack.

Put the card back on top.

3 Put the pack behind your back and pretend to shuffle the cards. Instead, just move the chosen card to the bottom of the pack.

I am shuffling the cards.

4 Hold the pack in front of you so you can see the card that is at the bottom (but your friend doesn't see what you are looking at).

5 Now you know the card, so your aim is to confuse your friend!

6 Take any card from the pack and say triumphantly **"Is this your card?"** Your friend won't be impressed, it's the wrong card!

7 Look disappointed and apologetic. Put the pack of cards behind your back again. This time shuffle the cards.

8 Place the cards on the table face up in six or seven small packs. Discreetly spot where the right card is.

9 Dramatically lay your hands above the packs in search of the card. Discard four or five packs.

10 Lay your hands above the remaining packs and discard all but the one containing the chosen card.

11 Place the remaining cards on the table face up, and lay your hands above the cards.

12 Make your hands shake dramatically when your hand is above the right card. Pick it up and say 'Is this your card?'

Tip
Be as dramatic as you like! When pretending to look for the card, you could use a spoon or another object of your choice to 'track' the card.

Card trick 2

Make all the cards apart from the summary cards into a pack. Put the pack of cards close to you on the table.

In one hand, hold the card that represents your cousins.

In the other, hold three cards representing your sister and two other members of your family.

Return these cards to the top of the pack as you tell the following story.

My sister is in her bedroom

...with my brother...

...my grandparents...

...and my cousins.

Everybody starts to argue with each other.

So, my cousins go into the sitting room.

My grandparents go into the kitchen.

And my brother goes into the garden.

So, I take out my magic wand: 'Abracadabra! Come back into my sister's room.'

I hear a noise on the stairs.

Someone knocks on the door.

I see my cousins...

...my grandparents...

...my brother!

Read how it's done on the opposite page.

How it's done

At the beginning, when you prepare the cards, discreetly take three random cards that you hide behind the card that represents the cousins.

What you place at the top of the pack is in fact six cards (the brother, the grandparents and the cousins + three random cards).

The cards that are moved further down the pack are the random cards. The brother, the grandparents and the cousins are still at the top of the pack.

Word list

in my sister's bedroom	I hear a noise on the stairs
with my brother	someone knocks on the door
my grandparents	I see
my cousins	
a big argument	
sitting room	
kitchen	
garden	
my magic wand	
come back	

Tip You could make up more stories with other cards.

At the farm, there is a sheep, a goat, a duck and a rabbit. A big wolf arrives and eats the sheep, the goat, the duck and the rabbit. But here's the good fairy with her magic wand. Abracadabra! The rabbit, the duck, the goat and the sheep are back again!

On my bed, there are my trousers, my shirt, my socks and my cap. My dog arrives and puts my trousers and my shirt in the toilet, my socks in the kitchen and my cap in the sitting room. But here's the good fairy with her magic wand. Abracadabra! And here back on my bed are my cap, my socks, my shirt and my trousers!

Word list

English

aeroplane
apple

baby
bicycle
boat
brother
bus

cap
car
card
cherry
chicken
clothes
cloud
cousins
cow
crocodile

duck

elephant

family
farm animals
father
fruit

giraffe

gloves
goat
grandparents
grapes

hippopotamus
horse

jacket

lion
lorry

mother
motorbike

orange

peach
pear
pig
pineapple
polar bear
pyjamas

rabbit
rain
rhino

sheep

shirt
shoes
sister
sky
snow
socks

strawberry
sun

thunderstorm
train
transport
trousers
twins

weather
wild animals
wind

zebra

Fruit

Fruit

Fruit

Cut these cards out carefully along the dotted line.

Fruit

Fruit

Fruit

Fruit

Fruit

Fruit

Fruit

grapes

Fruit

pineapple

Fruit

pear

Fruit

peach

Fruit

apple

Fruit

orange

Fruit

cherry

Fruit

strawberry

Wild animals

Wild animals

Wild animals

Wild animals

Wild animals

Wild animals

Wild animals

Wild animals

Wild animals

Wild animals

zebra

Wild animals

rhinoceros

Wild animals

lion

Wild animals

giraffe

Wild animals

elephant

Wild animals

crocodile

Wild animals

hippopotamus

Wild animals

polar bear

Farm animals

Farm animals

Farm animals

Cut these cards out carefully along the dotted line

Farm animals

Farm animals

Farm animals

Farm animals

Farm animals

Farm animals

Farm animals

chicken

Farm animals

pig

Farm animals

cow

Farm animals

sheep

Farm animals

horse

Farm animals

duck

Farm animals

rabbit

Farm animals

goat

Weather

Weather

Weather

Weather

Cut these cards out carefully along the dotted lines

Weather

Weather

Weather

Weather

Weather

Weather

Weather

rain

Weather

sun

Weather

cloud

Weather

wind

Weather

thunder-
storm

Weather

snow

Weather

sky

Weather

fog

Family

Family

Family

Family

Family

Family

Family

Family

Family

Family

grand-
parents

Family

brother

Family

sister

Family

mother

Family

father

Family

baby

Family

cousins

Family

twins

Clothes

Clothes

Clothes

Cut these cards out carefully along the dotted line

Clothes

Clothes

Clothes

Clothes

Clothes

Clothes

Clothes

trousers

Clothes

shirt

Clothes

shoes

Clothes

gloves

Clothes

pyjamas

Clothes

jacket

Clothes

cap

Clothes

socks

Transport

Transport

Transport

Cut these cards out carefully along the dotted line

Transport

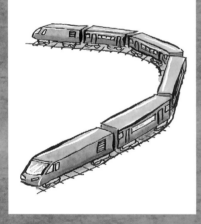

Transport

Transport

Transport

Transport

Transport

Transport

car

Transport

bicycle

Transport

train

Transport

boat

Transport

aeroplane

Transport

motorbike

Transport

lorry

Transport

bus

Summary cards

Cut these cards out carefully along the dotted lines.

Fruit

grapes

pineapple

peach

pear

apple

orange

cherry

strawberry

Wild animals

zebra

rhinoceros

lion

giraffe

elephant

crocodile

hippopotamus

polar bear

Farm animals

pig

cow

sheep

horse

duck

chicken

rabbit

goat

Weather

sun

cloud

rain

wind

thunderstorm

snow

sky

fog

Family

brother

sister

father

mother

grandparents

baby

cousins

twins

Clothes

shirt

shoes

gloves

pyjamas

jacket

trousers

cap

socks

Transport

bicycle

train

car

boat

aeroplane

motorbike

lorry

bus

INDUSTRIAL RAILWAYS IN COLOUR

A
Railway Bylines Special

Copyright IRWELL PRESS Ltd.,

ISBN 1-903266-14-9

*First published
in 2003 by Irwell Press Ltd.,
59A, High Street, Clophill,
Bedfordshire MK45 4BE
Printed by Newton Printing*

The first special colour book from Irwell Press (publishers of British Railways Illustrated – 'BRILL' magazine), was 'British Railways in Colour No.1' which appeared in 1999 and looked at main line locomotives and railways. Following the success of that volume and subsequent ones in the series, and of BRILL's companion magazine *Railway Bylines* (which regularly features industrial railways in its pages) there seemed to be scope for an 'industrial' sister book. So here we have Irwell's first colour survey of the industrial railway scene. Using large format (2½ inch square) colour transparencies, taken exclusively on Agfa film by Adrian Booth, the survey principally features steam traction, but also incorporates a representative selection of interesting diesels. The photographs are presented in geographical order, beginning in the north east of England, then working their way down through the Midlands and home counties to London and the south-east, then along the south coast, continuing around the south-west, looking at both south and north Wales, and then up through Lancashire and Cumbria, to finish in Scotland.

The author would like to acknowledge Allan C. Baker, Bob Darvill, Chris Down, Guthrie Hutton, Colin Mountford, Don Townsley, and Frank Jux, who have provided certain information contained within the captions. Dates referring to preserved locomotives are accurate as at January 2002. **Adrian Booth**

Right. 56 of the BR Western Region 'Paxman' locomotives were built at Swindon Works, emerging between July 1964 and October 1965. Numbered D9500 to D9555, they were 0-6-0 diesel hydraulics, fitted with six cylinder engines capable of developing 650hp at 1,500rpm. Generally unpopular with BR crews, the branch line traffic for which they were intended rapidly dried up and, incredibly, examples were placed in store by 1966. The first to be withdrawn was in December 1967, and the whole class was out of service by April 1969. These practically new, barely run-in locos, were quickly snapped up by private industry and almost the whole class was bought at a fraction of the cost of buying new. A few went to cement and oil companies, but seventeen were sold to the NCB, and twenty-three to Stewarts & Lloyds Ltd. The last-named used their new fleet for trip-working iron ore trains on their extensive rail networks in the Midlands, at Buckminster, Glendon, Harlaxton, and Corby. They were an outstanding success – on 8 November 1975, number 52 (D9537) is in typical action hauling an iron-ore train from Prior's Hall Quarry to Corby steelworks.

Although ordered as Ministry of Supply No.71463, Andrew Barclay W/No.2212 of 1946 was actually sold direct from its builders to the LNER, being ex-works on 9 July 1946. Classified J94, it ran as No.68078 on British Railways, working from Immingham, Thornaby and Langwith Junction sheds, prior to withdrawal in 1963. It was sold in March 1963 for use in private industry, going to Derek Crouch (Contractors) Ltd's coal disposal point at Widdrington in Northumberland (OS grid reference NZ 237957) where it received running number L2, but retained its original BR number. By the mid-1970s it was the last steam locomotive in commercial use in Northumberland, but thereafter was stored until leaving in October 1987 for preservation. It was a standard 'Austerity' 0-6-0 saddle tank, fitted with 18in x 26in inside cylinders and 4ft 3in diameter wheels and, when photographed on 4 November 1985, was keeping company (right) with ex-BR diesel shunter No.12052.